andrea

Keep on

Sharing God's Love

---

and be blessed

R. J. Bragg

Feb. 17, 2018

WESTBOW·
PRESS
A DIVISION OF THOMAS NELSON
& ZONDERVAN

WestBow Press books may be ordered through booksellers or by contacting:

WestBow Press
A Division of Thomas Nelson & Zondervan
1663 Liberty Drive
Bloomington, IN 47403
www.westbowpress.com
1 (866) 928-1240

ISBN: 978-1-4908-7399-2 (sc)
ISBN: 978-1-4908-7400-5 (hc)
ISBN: 978-1-4908-7398-5 (e)

Library of Congress Control Number: 2015904331

Print information available on the last page.

WestBow Press rev. date: 04/27/2015

CONTENTS

This book is dedicated to my family and friends, who believed in my dream. Yes, it was *you* who inspired me to continue to write; now I give you my finished work.

Each of us has been given the power
to share God's love!

God has given me these messages to share with
you what He wants each of us to do.

A PRAYER FOR THIS DAY!

(Received in meditation with my Lord on December 8, 2008)

Thank You, Lord, for this day that
You have given me. Thank You for my
life, my health, and all my strength.

I want to do Your will this day. You
have chosen me to do something
special that only I can do.

As I walk the path You have given me this day, I will enjoy Your grace, mercy, and truth, and I will keep Your covenant and testimonies forever.

Amen.

PREFACE

Sharing God's Love is about a journey we all will take as we live each day of our lives on this earth. Within these pages, I share God's love, starting with the birth of Jesus.

My Lord gave me these stories at different times when I was in meditation with Him. I do not expect anyone to find that he or she too is traveling on the same road this book presents, but if by chance you feel that there is a coincidence or similarity to your life, congratulations.

The first chapter is about how babies bring God's love and the association with how Jesus brings God's love to us. Next, "Following by Faith" shows the direction we all are to take. Once we have accepted Jesus as our Lord and Savior, then we are following by faith His direction for our lives.

You may not think it now, but as you read the Bible daily and understand it more, you will realize there have been moments in your life when you've received second chances.

It is my hope that reading this book will increase your faith so you can make good choices. Then when you are with others, Christian and non-Christian, you will be prepared to keep the Devil on the outside. It is only then that you will better understand what Jesus meant when he said we are to resist the Devil.

Jesus died for our sins. When we accept Him as our Lord and Savior, He comes to live within each of us and brings with Him the Holy Spirit, prosperity, health, and peace, to name a few. Now if you meet others who claim to be Christians but all they share with you is their sickness, this is a hint that they are not on the same course you are with your Lord and Savior. Be grounded, and be that light for them to see.

As your walk with Jesus grows, you will begin to understand His concern for your life when it comes to how you think about things. The best lesson is yet to come: when you learn that what God wants is for you to always allow your lamp to shine so others can see your good works and glorify Him. From this lesson, you will also realize that you came into this world naked and will leave the same.

As you enjoy your journey through this book, you will learn that what your Lord and Savior has given you will come to an end and He will call you to come home. All each of us can do is live each day as if it's the only one we have, and if by chance another day does arrive, we should thank God and give Him the glory for it.

Yes, this book is meant to be a blessing to each of you. I thank God that He gave me this message to share with you. Now as I keep my lamp shining, please keep yours too.

Tell a friend about this book, and we all can believe that our Lord and Savior is alive and waiting for all to come home and walk on the streets of gold.

God is love, and we are to carry God's love with us always, to be given away to all we come in contact with.

The gospel of John and the first letter of John both talk about the divine love God has for each of us.

The day you were born and the day you will die do not matter. It is what you do between your birth and death that determines where you spend eternity.

Babies Bring God's Love

Do you realize that today babies are the first to share God's love with us on earth? Just consider the birth of Jesus Christ. He was the first that I know of to share godlike love with each of us.

Now will you agree with me that all the godlike love that originated from God through babies and to us upon their arrival is by the power of our Lord and Savior?

1

Just think: a newborn baby is carried for nine months in the belly of his or her mother and then arrives here on earth to introduce each of us to God's love. I think that is powerful!

More than likely we all have heard the story of the baby Jesus coming into the world born of a virgin. The story also tells us about how the shepherds waited in the fields and then the angel guided them to see the baby Jesus and to receive God's love.

This same Jesus later died for our sins, and His love is with each of us today. And to think you may have never thought of it this way, that God used a baby to share His divine love with us. So why wouldn't God use babies today?

I'm sure we can agree we need all the love we can get. Therefore, let us agree for the purposes of this chapter that all babies are God's messengers who bring love.

Let's go further and say that the noises babies make while lying in their cribs are an expression of God's love. This baby language is their way of talking to us about God's love. As adults, we think we know it all when the truth of the matter is we are not listening to our babies. Because we are not listening, all we want to do is put them in their beds so we can get our much-needed rest. We should be listening to them when they make these noises and learning about godlike love.

Here is an excellent opportunity for us to realize that babies are speaking to us, but we blow it, even though all we have to do is take the time out of our busy schedules to listen and talk back to them.

Have you ever thought about what these precious bundles of joy are saying when they make all that noise to us? We don't know, and we choose not to listen.

We may be aware of how blessed all parents are when their bundles of joy arrive, but we must realize as well that babies are also blessed to be arriving. So why can't we believe that babies are telling us about God's love? After all, love is the *most* powerful emotion in the world. We can be sure the Devil does not want us to know that.

What babies could be saying to us may be as simple as "I'm bringing with me *love* to a world that does not have a factual

understanding of what love is all about."
Wouldn't that be profound? And what would
your response be if you understood this?

I'm sure anyone who hears those words
or who takes the time to really listen and
understand what any baby is saying would
be amazed.

Most of the time babies are lying down
making noise and talking to themselves.
It's those times that we are too busy doing
our own things. Maybe we are listening to
music, browsing the Internet, or talking on
the phone with a friend. Here is a special
moment missed when babies are telling
us something we need to know that could
change our lives and be a blessing to us.

Stop now, and reflect on the expression
"Take time to smell the roses." What are

roses? They are flowers created by God, a gift of love from the Almighty. Babies are a gift too, and that is why you need to take time to hear what these babies are saying.

Sometimes the conversation does not end there, and the baby could also be saying, "I am here to share love with everyone I meet."

Sharing God's love is babies' appointed purpose. At the time of their birth, we don't know what to expect. Yet the moment they arrive, they start making all kinds of noises. They are excited to share their journeys with us.

Let's imagine that they have left an environment of complete peace and that, before those nine months they were waiting to come to you, they were enjoying their relationship with our Father, His Son, and the Holy Spirit.

It is only when they are due to arrive here on earth that their purpose is manifested and they come bearing God's love to humanity.

Before their arrival, I believe all babies are surrounded by love, which they bring with them. It is only here on earth that they get to share God's love. What a precious blessing for everyone!

Babies spend their first year here with their earthly family and friends. During this period all they can do is share God's love with everyone who will listen. They enjoy special moments with anyone who provides them care.

In the meantime, during their first year they are also learning how to live in this new world and share God's love at the same time. Could this be why everyone loves babies? After all, they come to bring God's love.

We have limited our thoughts when it comes to babies to be *They are so cute* or *A baby is only a baby.* Now we can change those thoughts to *Do babies really go out and share their love with others?* Maybe this is where we fail, by not believing what God is capable of doing, let alone believing what any baby that comes from the Father is capable of doing. None of us really understands all the Almighty has for us. Maybe we need to listen to babies more and learn.

Let's start believing babies were born to share godlike love. After all, who doesn't love a baby? So don't let lack of faith prevent you from being successful with babies. We can begin with what we have learned.

What a revelation it is to become conscious of this manner of love from a baby; you may have never heard of this before, yet what you are receiving from all babies, believe it or not, is actually from God through the Holy Spirit.

What will babies discover when they begin to explore this new world. Based on our experiences in the world, we may have pessimistic outlooks for our babies. When all we can do is trust and believe. By knowing the Father, who cannot do anything wrong. We have to believe our babies are going to be all right.

All we have to do is share God's love back to them. This will strengthen them to follow the path the Father has given them. We may want to spare them from experiencing obstacles, especially because we know from our own experiences how bad obstacles in life can be but our babies will get through it, by the grace of God. We have to remember that we are to let go and let God.

Somehow, we believe we are babies' protectors on earth, when the truth of the matter is God is their protector. All we have to do is accept this, follow His Son, believe, and make sure our babies learn to do likewise.

Babies let us know their needs by crying out. These babies may be experiencing obstacles they had never experienced where they came from. And all we need to do is just love them, hold them, and talk to them. This will give them the reassurance they need for that moment.

Only when someone lovingly comes to a baby's rescue is he or she able to stop crying. As adults, our first reaction to babies' cries may be to feed them, change their diapers, pat them on their little backs, or hug them. Yes, they need all that, but babies desire love too, and as soon as we show our love, they immediately shower us with smiles as they give back their love.

It is love that babies know to give us, and we make them very happy when we show our love back. Our comforting words and expressions of love whispered in their little ears allow them to exude joy and laughter.

Every baby carries love that can be felt everywhere they go. As a child of God, a baby is sent to this world to be loved and to give love. The amount of love babies bring cannot be measured. When babies come into this world, all they know is that they are bringing love and need love to survive.

However, when it's time for a baby to leave this earth, at any age, he or she will not carry any unused love back to the Father. Jesus came bringing love, and He left His love back here for us to share with others. Babies do the same. They leave all the love they brought so we can continue giving our love to one another. Babies also come to this world to remind us that we too are God's babies, no matter how old we are.

We may not know why a baby is showing sadness, but we all can believe that somehow babies have their way of showing it. At those sad moments all we can do is show our love toward them.

Babies can show sadness when the people in their lives do not understand the importance of God's love. Here's a question for you: Are you living with godlike love in your life and passing it on to everyone?

Babies do grow up, and parents enroll them in school. What a joy the very first day is when they meet some of the children they knew before coming into this world. Do you remember your first day at school? Did you know many of those children?

Your parents left you in an unfamiliar area, and you may have cried. When you then saw someone you knew, maybe a cousin or the child living down the street or in the next apartment, how did you feel? Did you stop crying and feel more secure after seeing someone familiar?

Babies come to this unfamiliar place, the world, and don't feel the love they used to, the love they want and need. Love is the only laughter they understand. This is why they are so happy to see other children of God and can relate to them in their laughter and communicate with them, learning about what has been happening in their friends' lives.

Some of these children may have forgotten what godlike love is after coming to this world. How about you? Have you forgotten godlike love? Even if you have been here twenty-five years or longer, it is important for all babies and each of us to receive godlike love. It keeps all babies' and our supply of love in full measure.

After seeing their newfound friends who have been depleted of their own love supply, babies will gather around one another to make sure the love supply is replenished.

It is that simple. God is love, and He wants us to love. Jesus replied: 'Love the Lord your God with all your heart and with all your soul and with all your mind.' This is the first and greatest commandment. And the second is like it: 'Love your neighbor as yourself.' (Matthew 22:37–39, NIV.) Stop now and think about how you felt or would feel without love, and then think about how babies and all children might feel without love. Yes, it must be disappointing for anyone who comes into this world and does not feel or receive any love from their parents, grandparents, siblings, aunts, uncles, and friends of the family, especially considering what it was like before coming into this world.

The next time you see a group of children playing, stop and watch them to see the godlike love being shared. Now you know why they gather around their newfound friends—to replenish this love. Some of these children have never received godlike love from their parents, friends, or extended families.

Hopefully now you understand the importance of this love since their arrival. There are some babies who have died because they did not receive this godlike love from their families or friends. Love is a very important element in our lives. When you read God's Word, you will understand more about the love that you brought and that all babies continue to bring to this world when they are born.

This love is more than enough for our lives while here, and we will be able to leave some of it behind when we die. Is that so hard to believe? This is why I think love is so important to us. Let's love the Lord as He loves us and love one another likewise.

All that I ask of you is to never stop loving babies or anyone else so this world can be better for all babies and for each of us.

In summary, what keeps babies going while here with us is godlike love. Babies are able to carry God's love with them at all times. Just knowing that God is love and that babies get to leave God's love here on earth when they leave this world is in itself reason enough to want to love even more.

Babies just want to love us so much that all we have to do is love back. Always remember it is God's love that makes it happen.

Now faith is the substance of things hoped for, the evidence of things not seen.

—Hebrews 11:1 (KJV)

FOLLOWING BY FAITH

The story of Moses in the book of Exodus and the coming of Immanuel, the Savior, in Isaiah 7:14 reveal God's escape plan from enslavement. Moses and Immanuel are both profound examples of God's plan for rescuing humanity. God's escape plan is also written throughout the Bible for each of us to know and follow.

In Moses' day, God freed the Israelites from the Egyptian captors (Exodus 12:31). The

New Testament relates God's plan to free people from sin. The rescuer is His only Son, Jesus, whom He sent to earth to free those in slavery. His goal for humankind was eternal life.

I believe God is asking each of us, why don't you believe Jesus came to free you of any oppression? All we have to do is follow Him by faith. The Bible says our faith should be like a mustard seed: "...If you have faith as a grain of mustard seed, ye shall say unto this mountain; Remove hence to yonder place; and it shall remove; and nothing shall be impossible unto you" (Matthew 17:20 KJV). And as Christians, our faith should always be growing, which we can accomplish by reading the Word.

Our faith is also about our love. God asks us to love one another, but somehow not all of us are doing that. I believe God is asking each of us to trust Him for our release from captivity. God asks us *all* to feed the hungry, but only some of us are. God also asks us to visit the sick; when was the last time you did that?

In a wonderfully miraculous way, we are free to serve Him as we take care of others. Feeding? Yes. Nursing? Yes. Nurturing? Yes. None of these are hard to accomplish when we first accept His escape plan.

God asks us to visit those in prison. Have you done this? If those who claimed to be Christians would simply do most of the above, we all would live in a better world because we would be following by faith.

Answer this question: Why are only a few of us doing what God asks?

All you have to do is look around and see those who are suffering. I know you could say, "All are suffering." You would be right somewhat, but now is a good time to examine ourselves to see if we are being faithful Christians toward those God has put on our path.

Jesus came and brought His Word to each of us. The first step is to repent of any past sins. Yes, we all have sinned. The next step is to follow Christ by faith. Our new beginning is always doing what the Father has asked us. Doing so will create a better world for Christ to come back to.

The Bible says He is coming back! The question now is, do you have the faith to believe He will? If so, are you ready for His return?

Do you want to see Jesus now, or are you waiting until you are truly ready for His return? And do you know when that will be?

When He comes back, let's hope we'll all be ready and none of us will be like the five virgins who had to go find more oil in the parable of the ten virgins (see Matthew 25:1–13). The bridegroom came while they were gone, and they missed him because they didn't have everything they needed to come in and be with Him. Jesus does not want you to go through your life like this.

To be ready today, you have to take some action. Then follow your action so that when Jesus does come, you will be ready. Just remember that not being ready is not following by faith.

When you are following Jesus daily, the Holy Spirit touches your heart and tells you what you are to do; at the end of each day you can rejoice over what you did and give God the glory.

When you are following by faith, you sleep better. Some of you will discover that sickness will abandon you. It will cease from taking the first priority in your life.

We all can learn how to follow by faith using Paul's words in 2 Timothy 4:7–8 NIV ("I have fought the good fight, I have finished the race. I have kept the faith. Now there is in store for me the crown of righteousness, which the Lord, the righteous Judge, will award to me on that day – and not only to me, but also to all who have longed for his appearing.") Why don't you say this Scripture as you get ready every day to be with the Lord?

The key to living and following by faith then becomes an everyday thought. You cannot allow the Enemy to deceive you. Therefore, what you can do now is designate the next thirty days to make Jesus first in your life. You will not know the value of doing this until you try. Following Jesus by faith could be the richest thing you have ever done.

At the end of those thirty days, if you are not satisfied, you still have the option to stop following Jesus. It's your choice because you can always go back to following Satan.

*Always remember, loving
God should come first!*

What each of us must learn about
the people in our lives is that they
can give us only second best when
it comes to love. When it comes to
love, first best comes from *God*!

THANK GOD FOR
SECOND CHANCES

Every day God gives you a second chance.
Second chances are God's way of sharing
His love with you again. In this chapter,
I will share common examples of second
chances from God.

As we look back on our lives, we should be
able to admit that God does give second
chances. If by chance you did not do
what you wanted to do today, tomorrow

is your second chance. This blessing is not something you want to ignore; take advantage of it.

I have heard stories about and known people who had a heated argument with a loved one and neither told the other he or she was sorry before going to sleep. How sad that they did not know what the Word of God says in Ephesians 4:26 NIV: "Do not let the sun go down while you are still angry." Yet the two went to bed in their wrath. It was by the grace of God that they had a second chance the next day.

Either one could have sought forgiveness by saying I'm sorry, but neither did. It's always better if both ask for forgiveness. In doing so, God would show them His love. However, despite going to bed angry, the next day each was able to experience God's love and a second chance.

It is thanks to God that they each lived to experience a second chance. One could have died during the night. In this case, God sharing His love made it possible for the two to have a second chance.

As another example, when people are diagnosed with an illness, almost everyone immediately prays first. When things start to go bad, our first words are "Oh, God, help me." But these words should have been on our lips before. If you knew 1 Peter 2:24 KJV, you would say, "By whose stripes ye were healed."

We have a loving God who is there all the time waiting for His Word to help. When we repent of any worldly sins and believe in our hearts that God is there to answer all prayers, we will receive our second chances.

In Ezekiel 18:30, God was there for the land of Israel, and He is here for you today. God loves you and does not want any of His children to perish (2 Peter 3:9). Always remember that it's your choice whether to receive the second chance.

Why can't the words from your mouth today and always be "Thank God I'm healed"? To add to your healing, say, "I have recuperated from my illness. Things are going well, and I won't ever forget from whence my second chance came."

God is here to assist you every day. This is why He sent his Son, Jesus Christ, and, when His Son left earth, the Holy Spirit came. So all that is left for us to do now is keep our minds focused on Him daily and live in the first chance while also knowing that God can give second chances.

For God so loved the world, that he gave his only begotten Son, that whosoever believeth in him should not perish, but have everlasting life.

—John 3:16 (KJV)

KEEPING THE DEVIL
ON THE OUTSIDE

Isn't it alarming to be living at a time when so much evil abounds? All Christians are blessed with the Word of God; His Son, Jesus Christ; and the Holy Spirit. Yet we are living in a world dominated by evil. Why is it that we fail to display to the world that Jesus died on the cross for our sins?

We have to reckon with ourselves and realize that without the living Christ the

Enemy will steal our strength and faith. We have to be strong in our belief and seek Christ's direction for our lives daily. To live with the Devil on the outside, perhaps you have to read the Bible to be inspired by God with His Word?

Hopefully this chapter will help you see clearly a way to live with the Devil on the outside.

The Bible tells us to "resist the devil" (James 4:7 NIV) and to "put on the whole armor of God to stand against the wiles of the devil" (Ephesians 6:11 KJV). If you plan on living your life without God's Word, especially in these times, then you have no idea what it takes to keep the Devil on the outside.

I'd like to share with you a little about myself and how I keep the Devil on the outside of my life. I was baptized at age twelve and confirmed in the Episcopal Church in Petersburg, Virginia. After living in Washington, DC, for ten years, I stepped out in faith and moved to Chicago, Illinois at the age of 29.

Wanting more and knowing I had it in me, I moved again to Dallas, Texas, to attend Bishop College. Still keeping the Devil on the outside, I did very well at Bishop and was on the dean's list.

While I sought a church in Dallas, God led me to many different churches until I found my home at St. Christopher's Episcopal Church. I would travel miles on Sunday mornings to worship there. It was here that a member suggested the University of Texas in Arlington (UTA) to me.

Looking back, I know that I was being led by the Holy Spirit, and thank God I kept the Devil on the outside.

I graduated from UTA in 1979 in the field of my dream at that time, architectural/ interior design. I traveled back to Chicago. I was unable to secure employment there, so I left for a job at a successful firm in Oklahoma City.

It was in Oklahoma City (OKC) at the age of 39 I received the Baptism of the Holy Spirit and began speaking in tongue. I can truly say now from this experience, my belief to keeping the Devil on the outside increased. I also started attending a Wednesday-night Bible study.

The church I was attending had a wonderful teaching minister who was adamant when it came to using God's Word. His favorite Scripture was "By His stripes you are healed" (1 Peter 2:24 KJV). In his messages he was always stressing the importance of keeping the Devil out of your life.

At first I did not know what he meant, but after attending services every Wednesday night, I began to comprehend a little more about how I could really keep the Devil out of my life. I absorbed what this minister was saying based on Scriptures and started to apply what I heard. Standing on God's Word bolstered my spirit tremendously!

I can now confess that when it comes to my life, I know what it takes to keep the Devil on the outside. It's that simple: I have learned to stay focused on Jesus Christ and the Word of God daily.

I have broadened my understanding of the Word by reading the Bible and Christian books and listening to Christian preachers and other Christian leaders. Through some of these teachings I've learned that some verses should not be taken literally.

When you apply God's truths, you will not be trapped in the common assumption that His Word is contradictory when it's not!

I am aware that not everyone will do what I did to gain an understanding and to become faithful regarding keeping the Devil on the outside. Some, however, will apply this process and will experience success. I can only write that for me and my life I keep the Devil on the outside and do not receive sickness in my body or claim any sickness.

I now understand that receiving sickness and showing sickness are two different things. You may see a person showing symptoms of sickness, but that does not always mean the person is sick. You have to understand that what's going on with him or her has nothing to do with what you can see. Allowing this to become a measuring point for your life may just help you to keep the Devil on the outside.

When you follow by faith the Word of God, you can respect others beliefs. So the next time you meet a person who looks sick to you but says, "By His stripes I am healed," remember this person believes he or she is well because of his or her faith.

To keep the Devil on the outside, believe and take lessons from other people. If you don't believe you can be healed by the Word of God, you can learn from others how you too can live by faith. The Word of God says, "Death and life are in the power of the tongue: and they that love it shall eat the fruit thereof" (Proverbs 18:21 KJV).

The reason I do not personally claim or receive any symptoms of sickness is based on my understanding of God's Word for my life at this time.

I can only entreat you to begin today reading God's Word for your life and to allow the Holy Spirit to be your guide to a healthier understanding.

I am sharing what I have learned and believe for my life because I believe it will work for you too. Only once you apply the Word of God for you will anything I have said work for you.

Two people not seeing the same thing can both think they are right in their own mind's eye. They will both need to develop that oneness with the Word of God in their lives for any solution to have a win-win effect for their lives.

I believe strongly that when a person claims any symptoms of sickness, the Devil is the first to rejoice. I also believe claiming these symptoms is a sure sign that your faith level in God's promises is a little low and needs to be upgraded by reading His Word.

Claiming sickness could also be a sign that you have fallen out of God's grace and are living in the world's deathtrap. Jesus' death on the cross was the answer to keeping you out of such a situation.

Take the time *now* to begin reading God's Word so you can keep the Devil outside of your life. Whenever the Devil comes around with sickness, I make it a big point to let him know that I claim God's healing power by repeating the Scripture as Jesus taught us, and then the Devil flees. I also offer him the blood of Jesus, and for sure he will leave.

Resist the devil, and he
will flee from you.
—James 4:7 (KJV)

Greater is he that is in you,
than he that is in the world.
—1 John 4:4 (KJV)

WHY SHARE SICKNESS WHEN YOU CAN SHARE LOVE?

In this chapter I hope to explain why people always want to share sickness with you and not their love.

The first reason is sharing sickness is easy. It is conversation, and we all want to talk with someone. This may well be true, but there are lots of things we can talk about besides sickness.

We can always share Jesus Christ with people. He woke you up this morning. You could share that and what you have experienced since waking up—the people you have met or seen and talked with since awakening. If you read your Bible, you can share what you read and what you got from the Word.

Reading (Matthew 4:23, 9:35, and 10:1) convey to me that Jesus went out healing all manner of sickness. Then in Matthew 8:17 NIV, "He took up our infirmities and carried our diseases"

This information alone is grounds for anyone to confess he or she is well. There is no rationale for people to share their sickness and not their love.

This is also why I believe that sickness is a lie from the Devil. God's Word does not give us sickness. So when I read "By whose strips ye were healed" (1 Peter 2:24 KJV), I am led to trust that God will heal anyone who claims His promises instead of claiming his or her sickness.

The next time you are tempted to say "I'm sick," instead say "By His Stripes I am healed" or "No weapon formed against me will prosper." I believe that by doing this you are giving God the glory while at the same time letting the Holy Spirit remove the arrows Satan has shot into your body.

God does not make us sick to get us well. However, in the book of Job, we learn that God did allow Job to be tested. He did so to prove to us Job's faithfulness. Ordinarily, God does not play games with

His children. He created us well. The Bible is our guide, prescription, and manual for living well and staying healthy.

To accept Jesus Christ as your Lord and Savior, you must read His Word, the Bible. Then He will send the Holy Spirit to live within you, giving you the freedom to do what only the Holy Spirit can do for your life as you walk the path God has given you.

Now stop being your own worst enemy, and read James 3:1–10 in your Bible when you have the time to discover what James says about the tongue? Then in James 4:7, NIV, it reads: "Resist the devil, and he will flee from you." These two Scriptures are bullets you can shoot at the Devil when he sends sickness your way.

On the other hand, always remember that when you least expect it, the Devil is lurking in the background waiting to trip you up. You have to begin resisting the Devil and speaking God's Word now so the Holy Spirit can come to your recue!

The choice is yours. If you choose to invoke sickness, please keep it to yourself; no one wants to hear about your maladies, about your being sick with this or that. Instead start sending God's love to everyone.

When you speak God's words, others who hear them can receive them. Those words will become seeds that penetrate others' bodies to give them life and health.

Here's my challenge for you for the next twenty-one days: speak only God's healing words in your life.

If you complete the first twenty-one days and believe it is not working, just remember you still have another choice— for the next twenty-one days. You can be sick, but don't come around me with your knives because I am able to quench all the fiery darts of the wicked.

Beloved, let us love one another; for
love is of God; and every one that loveth
is born of God, and knoweth God.

He that loveth not knoweth
not God; for God is love.

In this was manifested the love of
God toward us, because God sent
his only begotten Son into the world,
that we might live through him.

Herein is love, not that we loved God,
but that he loved us, and sent his Son
to be the propitiation for our sins.

—1 John 4:7–10 (KJV)

ARE YOU THINKING ABOUT THINGS?

Why? And what things are you thinking about? Somehow we have allowed the world to dictate the way we should think. We have God, His Word, Jesus Christ, and the Holy Spirit to lead us in the way we should be thinking. With all that, why do we allow the world to decide how we are to think? The answers too many of your problems can be found if you accept Jesus Christ as your Savior.

The first step is becoming aware of what you are thinking about. Especially when it comes to what you think you are supposed to do and obtain while here on earth?

Next answer this question: Why do we, as adults, spend so much time thinking about what we have to do that we forget what it was like when we were babies coming into this world bringing God's love? We don't need to worry about what we have to do because through faith we have everything we need in this life.

Genesis 2:25 KJV says, "They were both naked, the man and his wife, and were not ashamed." You too came into this world naked. Then Ecclesiastes 5:15 KJV mentions that "naked shall he return to go as he came and shall take nothing." This implies that nothing will be in your hands when you leave this world. The question remains, are we spending our time thinking about unnecessary things, instead of about what the Father want us to do?

Reflect: Naked you came, and naked you leave, carrying nothing away with you. All the things you have purchased or acquired for your comfort will stay here for someone else to enjoy.

You came without and will depart empty handed also. Now ask yourself again, why do we spend so much time trying to accumulate so much?

Matthew 25:25 talks about the one who buried his talent (money), and Luke 18:18–23 talks of the rich ruler who left with his head down when Jesus said he should go and sell what he had and give to the poor. Maybe the rich ruler did not realize Jesus was telling him how he could get into the kingdom. Maybe this story is our lesson to become more aware of the things we think about.

The Bible speaks about having wealth and about giving to the poor. God has given us many jewels in His Word for us to live by. I believe that we are not to become so hung up on material possessions and forget God. We should be God's servants and work to bring the lost in Christ into the kingdom, where our rewards will be great for being good servants.

So stop spending all your time on getting stuff for others to enjoy after you have left this earth. God has many lessons in the Bible for you to follow; stuff is not one of them. In Matthew 6:19, Jesus tells us about storing up treasures on earth. Then in verse 20, He says to store up treasures in heaven.

Then there's the money you may skillfully hide in a book, under a chair, or behind a picture. It will become someone else's treasure when found, along with your favorite dress, suit, hat, or shoes. We can only hope that person will receive as many compliments as you did.

Too bad the things you acquire cannot enter heaven, where God is in charge. All the money and power you have on earth have no influence in heaven—that is, unless you use your money and power to help God's kingdom. Do you give your 10 percent? How about giving to the homeless? Do you teach a Christian educational class for the youth? All of these are helpful things you can do while on earth.

Today you can start changing what you think about and instead focus on what is needed to get into heaven. You will have your seat waiting for you when you arrive in heaven.

For God did not call us to
uncleanness, but in holiness.
—1 Thessalonians 4:7 (KJV)

A CALL FROM GOD

Do you remember your mother or father calling you by your whole name to come home? You knew instinctively that they meant "Right now!" When you hear God calling you to come home, it also will mean "Right now!" It will not be the same as your parents' call, and you will know that, somehow. No one else will hear this call.

Sooner or later each of us will get that call from God saying He is ready for us to come home—right now. We know this day is coming, but we think it's just not today.

When that day does come, you will not have time to pack a bag. Yes, you will have to leave just as you are! Your hair may need cutting, your nails may need a manicure, and yes, no time for any makeup. All I know is when the bridegroom comes, you must be ready.

Every day you are supposed to be doing just that, getting ready for the call from God. Now read the parable of the ten virgins in Matthew 25 to understand the meaning of the urges and the importance of being ready.

When you arrive to the throne room and witness all His worshippers, seeing how beautiful everyone is, you will forget about yourself. Your eyes will be widely opened to your surroundings.

The splendors around you, the white garments everyone is wearing, and the heavenly vista will be breathtaking to you, but the awakening will be from your heavenly Father, who will give you the power to enjoy every moment.

Once reality sets in, you will know that you are in His place, the one you read about. You are seeing it, and it is beyond anything you could have ever imaged.

Then you see the Father; His Son, Jesus Christ; and your loved ones. All this excitement! It's happening so fast! You will again forget about yourself. You look like everyone else, and this is what it is all about.

While you were on earth, you spent too much money doing your own thing. If you had only used some of your money and your time to help others, it would mean much more now than anything else you had done.

Now it is hitting you! Yes, you have made it into heaven, and now it is too late to help anyone. The only question you can ask yourself is, why do I deserve to be in heaven? The answer is because you accepted Jesus Christ as your Lord and Savior. Although you may not have lived every moment on earth doing God's will, you still get to come to heaven.

Why wasn't accepting and following Christ not explained more clearly to you as a churchgoing Christian? Were you so caught up in the world that you did not understand that the world is only for those in Satan's court?

James 4:7 KJV tells us "to resist the devil and he will flee from you." Most have read this verse, yet there are times we do not do what it says. Not believing these words is not for our glory. Resisting the Devil is an everyday job.

Then there are some who may think, *If I only had understood then, I could have done more for the less fortunate.* We somehow forget Jesus' words when He said "A new commandment I give unto you. That ye love one another; as I have loved you, that ye also love one another." (John 13:34 KJV). I hope this book will enlighten you to do more for humankind while you are living here on earth.

Always remember that we have more to give and not just to ourselves. (As it is written: "He has scattered abroad his gifts to the poor; his righteousness endures forever." 2 Corinthians 9:9).

You can now thank God that you understand John 3:16 and Romans 10 enough to get you into the throne room. We receive this blessing while on earth so we will be able to enjoy our arrival in heaven.

I hope this chapter helps you truly understand the importance of helping others while here on earth, because it is all for the glory of God. First Corinthians 3:8 says "The man who plants and the man who waters have one purpose, and each will be rewarded according to his own labor."

What you do in your life is called preparation, because He will be calling you. It is going to happen! You do not want to look back as you exit this earth and regret that you did not do more.

You have only one chance to make your arrival in heaven a great and joyful thanksgiving! That chance happens while on earth. Your life is meant to be your testimony for others. Make sure your life is a good influence for others. God wants everyone's arrival to heaven to be a joyful one.

Conclusion

Let today be the first day of your life in sharing God's love by your acceptance of His Son, Jesus Christ.

First open your heart unto Jesus. Ask Him to come in and be your Lord and Savior and to give you eternal life. Ask Him to remove all sins from your life so that you can walk the path that He has given you to walk.

Trust in Him and believe, and you will be saved.

I love you, my sisters and brothers.

Thank you for reading my first book.

I wish to leave you with this short poem.

RJ is my name,

Jesus Christ is my claim,

and the peace of the Lord is my gain!

I Love you!

This book is a result of my spending time with God and the Holy Spirit speaking to me while I sat on the floor in my prayer closet.

I heard these words in my spirit, so I wrote them down to really understand what was being said. Sometime later I realized that these words were not meant for me only but were to be passed on to others.

I now know that I am a lamp for God's use, and the Holy Spirit's job is to keep me plugged in.

Without the Word of God, the lightbulb in us, we are just lamps standing around in darkness.

CPSIA information can be obtained at www.ICGtesting.com
Printed in the USA
BVOW05s1756110515

399634BV00001BB/1/P

9 781490 873992